Volume 101 of the Yale Series of Younger Poets

Frail-Craft

Jessica Fisher

Foreword by Louise Glück

Yale University Press

New Haven & London

Designed by James J. Johnson and
set in Electra and Syntax Roman types by Keystone Typesetting, Inc.
Printed in the United States of America.

Library of Congress Cataloging-in-Publication Data

Fisher, Jessica.
Frail-craft / Jessica Fisher ; foreword by Louise Glück.
p.   cm. — (Yale series of younger poets ; v. 101)
ISBN 978-0-300-11032-6 (alk. paper)
ISBN 978-0-300-12235-0 (pbk. : alk. paper)
I. Title.
PS3606.I7755F73 2007
811'.6—dc22
2006030901

A catalogue record for this book is available from the British Library.

The paper in this book meets the guidelines for permanence and durability of the Committee on
Production Guidelines for Book Longevity of the Council on Library Resources.

10 9 8 7 6 5 4 3 2 1

for Dan
& Sylvie

CONTENTS

Foreword by Louise Glück   xi

Acknowledgments   xix

1

Journey   3

Lullaby   4

Love's Vicissitudes   5

A Riddle for the Body   6

Nonsight   7

    1. *Spiral Jetty*

    2. *Sun Tunnels*

    3. Canal

Memory Burn   10

June   11

The Borrowed Door   12

    1. Castaway

    2. Inscape

    3. Mislaid

Now—The Parade   16

2

The Wedding 21

West 12th Street 22

Three Dreams 23

Dream for My Other Brother 24

Errata 25

The Residual 26

Ten Boats 27

Love Cried Me a River 28

Love Letter 29

The Sermon 30

The Change 31

Flayed 32

3

Frail-Craft 35

Water, Voda 36

Looking for You in the *OED* 37

Song 38

Novella 39

The Promise of Nostos 45

The Right to Pleasure 46

Tide 47

Reckless 48

Brancusi's Heads 49

4

Debate   53

    1. Conjecture

    2. Against Conjecture

The Indistinguishability of Brothers   55

Reading to Know You   56

My Russian Lullaby   57

The Hunger for Form   58

Stereography   59

    1. Winter Expedition

    2. Downstream

    3. Augury

    4. Gorge

    5. View from Western Summit

    6. Half Stereograph of Fallen Leaf Lake

    7. Pioneer's Cabin, Near Grove

Notes   67

FOREWORD

The poet Peter Streckfus once remarked that what he loved most in a book of poems was a quality of persistent strangeness—"swimming in the confusion of it" was his phrase for the reader's initial experience. This quality makes, as Streckfus suggests, an environment; it is not a matter of the shrewdly confused surface or of opacity, nor can it be elaborated into a deliberate aesthetic. Rather one feels that something has been discovered in the language itself, some property or capacity, some tone never before transcribed, whose implicit meanings the poet has found ways to reveal.

Jessica Fisher writes a poetry of this kind, haunting, elusive, luminous, its greatest mystery how plain-spoken it is. Sensory impressions, which usually serve as emblems of or connections to emotion, seem suddenly in this work a language of mind, their function neither metonymic nor dramatic. They are like the dye with which a scientist injects his specimen, to track some response or behavior. Fisher uses the senses this way, to observe how being is converted into thinking. The poems move like dreams or spells: momentum, here, seems less a function of will than an evolved form of passivity; it is that condition in which freedom from decision and choice makes possible a unique flowering of attentiveness and reflection. The poems succumb to movement as though it were desire, with its obsessive repetitions and reenactments, its circularity:

> Because the valley spreads wide, ridged with the signs
> we read; or because what we needed was always at hand—
> reach down and there was a book, there a slipper, there a glass
> of ice cold water. Hopefully we walked
> the paths laid before us, there was a burr-bush,
> there a blue jay, quail and other creatures, too many

to follow. Where did they go once we lost their lead?
Which is to say, where did we not go? Quick, quick,
they called to us, but we heard only the sound
of our boots on dried leaves, and were mesmerized;
we spoke to one another of things in the path,
we chucked to our horses, when we had them,
and when we had hats we took them in our hands
and hallooed to the passersby (brahma bull, bright
green bird) though we were not yet out of the wood,
instead it closed in around us, deep were its streams
and the trees thick around and thick together. . . .

"Journey"

Impossible to begin discussion without first saying how beautiful a thing this is with its calm unfolding syntax, its air, common to so many of Fisher's poems, of being not exactly of this time—better perhaps to say not of time at all. This is time from a perspective not yet ours, time simultaneously infinite and momentary, the voice a continuity through mutability. Like Frost's "Directive," a poem it resembles in its dramatic situation (though the pairing is revelatory mainly in the differences it suggests), "Journey" seems to have slid off the map; it takes place either permanently, without beginning or end, or repeatedly—it takes place, that is, in myth time, in fairy-tale time. The alert floating voice is hard to anchor in a body, though it reports physical actions and sensations. The usual signals of age and gender are utterly absent. A sense of the child's voice comes and goes, but despite its intimacy, "Journey" is not a poem of personal history or personal dilemma. "What do you think we dreamt," this voice asks us toward the end, its casual familiarity transforming the reader from reader to companion. The answer reveals nothing of the dreamer's character: this is not a poem that seeks to identify motive or obsession, though like all poems of obsession, "Journey" is a ritual. But the catalyst is external, circumstantial. What initiates "Journey" is the fact that these paths exist: "laid before us," the poem says; they allude neither to goal nor to destination. The poem ends in dream; the dream recapitulates experience, which becomes increasingly impossible to separate from dream. Its meaning is not known, though its importance is not doubted.

Some poets conduct themselves as though they were directing traffic; with others one can hardly see any sign of imposed will. Fisher doesn't bully or coerce; her voice confides and drifts and veers, it pieces together impressions: no orders, no laying down of the law. The poems seem almost impersonal, as though their author were a sensibility, not a history. And yet, through even the most mysterious landscapes, this oddly jaunty voice, unplaceable yet distinctly human, this voice with its faintly archaic sound, periodically speaks.

The remarkable music of "Journey" characterizes Fisher's work; it doesn't indicate her range. Some of the best poems in *Frail-Craft* are prose poems. These eerie vignettes inhabit, simultaneously, the dreaming mind and the detached intelligence that operates intermittently within the dream. One of the book's four sections is composed entirely of these poems, but the gesture appears earlier, in the amazing poem that ends the first section like an exploding flock of balloons, a Fellini movie crossed with a very sophisticated children's book. It needs to be read in its entirety; no excerpt can give adequate sense of its ingenious shifts and surreal ebullience, though the opening lines convey something of both:

> Now—the parade. Lions, red, black & yellow. They *never* go anywhere without a drummer, & also have someone to carry extra oranges, & a hat carrier, for when they're tired. If their heads are bare they can be bonked with a stick. . . .

And much later, after many shifts:

> . . . yesterday the sun shone. Mounted police forced the dancers off the street. Really exciting. All the windows in the town were covered with screening for that very event. A good time was had by all. Good dinner, good people, good night.
> "Now—the Parade"

The mainly short poems of section two sustain these energies. They are, all of them, dreams, though they vary widely in their tones, their scenarios. This is a difficult form for poems: most poets seem a touch too proud of their dreams, too aware of their resonances. Fisher has found a way to use this material mainly, I think, because she never steps out of her invented worlds:

> —the dream I stayed with past waking
> in which Pascale sits sewing rabbit fur to glove your hands
> and silently, feet propped on a table, I flay a long strip
> from each thigh to make you boots. The skin peels easily,
> it's like stripping the pale bark from a fallen birch,
> the muscle beneath like the crimson trunk still teeming . . .
> "Flayed"

Or this:

> A long man came on foot, his hair was long too. He spoke above the river. Many people came, so many that his voice couldn't reach them all, but I heard it: I climbed a tree just behind.
> Below me, a woman got to her knees and cried, her hair was thin as a bird's first feathers, her mouth made a horrible shape.

Mother said she must be a sinner, that the words of this man, who has held the Christ, pricked her soul like a needle does cloth.

I didn't cry, nor did Daan Nachtegaal—he was in the tree too. After the man finished we went back to swordfighting. The sinners followed him into the river and drowned.

"The Sermon"

The elasticity of the form, the clarity and directness of this voice speaking from within contexts that seem fairly remote precincts of reality, allow Fisher to construct poems larger than might ordinarily seem within the range of a poet of such marked lyric temperament. As its title suggests, "Novella" is a miniature novel: in terms of plot, it begins with the disappearance of the hero. He stays vanished throughout, as though the function of the beloved were to lead the speaker back into imagination, which resurrects and perpetuates the connection. We collude, as readers, in his disappearance: if the wrong were righted, the poem would end. Whereas seeking him confirms his importance and intensifies his charisma. In this sense, "Novella" is also a poem *about* reading, about being lost in, a wanderer in, a text. "What you find when you're lost you can't look for," the poem tells us. The argument being, "you'd have to get lost to find it again." A logic both impeccable and perverse, deeply invested in the condition of being lost. As it did in "Journey," *seeking* in "Novella" means following a path that has been set or created, in this case by François, to François. We can't find him, and he can't get back: "His footsteps, left on the ice, would be gone when he went to retrace them." In these and other poems here, a particular kind of immersion figures: that being lost in which great discoveries are made, the center of one's being if not found at least approached. Always accident and chance are preferred to purpose. And the path, often, is "the lead that led astray." So that seeking, which recurs, seems not at odds with passivity, since chance and accident, like fate, cannot by definition be fixed objectives. Seeking is often being led; in *Frail-Craft* it alludes to depth, not distance.

For all the music, the sensuous detail of Fisher's art, her demeanor is essentially cool, measuring, intellectual—*speculative* may be a more accurate term. When such composure takes on, as it does in a number of shorter poems, explicitly passionate or erotic subjects, what results are poems so pure, so violent, so absolute, they seem like choral laments in Greek tragedy:

> You would think that I go mad with grief
> when the white sails fill and the keel cuts
> the waters like a knife honed on whetstone:
> that's the way you're taught to interpret these signs—

matted hair, the salt-dirt lines where sweat has run,
hands that feed the mouth but will not wipe it.
But when my love decides to go and then is gone,
I can still taste him, bitter in the throat; I still
feel the weight of his body as he fights sleep.
I do not fight it: on the contrary, I live there,
and what you see in me that you think grief
is the refusal to wake, that is to say, is pleasure:
qui donne du plaisir en a, and so if
when he couldn't sleep in that long still night
you sensed it and woke to show him how
to unfasten each and every button, then it is
promised you, even when he goes—

"The Right to Pleasure"

What is being in the world like? For American poets in the mid- to late twentieth century, this has meant, in the main, being in a single world patrolled by a single intelligence bent on finding meaning. The poems made by these compulsions have been essentially dramatic, artificially weighted at the end with insight. Impatience with these premises, with pat, histrionic endings, has fueled a poetry more interested in impressions and possibility than in symbols and conclusions. This poetry wants to explore experience before it becomes coherent, therefore too rigorously channeled.

In various ways, many contemporary poets try to inhabit the earliest possible phase of this process, the point before experience begins to be organized into categories. The willed intensity and inertia of emphatic closure has bred revulsion to any stage preliminary to, therefore tainted by, closure. Chaos has seemed increasingly fertile and attractive; the great problem is that chaos embodied in language is not chaos but form; the page cannot contain the void. This does not mean memorable poems have not been made of these ambitions. But such poems are an artifice in their own way, objects with boundaries, not the wind of the infinite.

The word *artifice* is very grim: it cannot suggest our experience of art, principally because it does not suggest the world of feeling which is both the source and object of art. Too often distaste for sentiment, anxiety at the limitations of the self, create contempt for feeling, as though feeling were what was left over after the great work of the mind was finished.

These issues obtain here, partly because Jessica Fisher has a marked taste for experiment: *Frail-Craft* inhabits the concerns of a period, its philosophic and linguistic dilemmas, but it does so with an intensity and suppleness I have rarely encountered: experiment never deteriorates into complacency.

Her poems are analytic meditations, their variety and beauty manifestations of extraordinary sensitivity to English syntax. She shares with her contemporaries intelligent suspicion of worn forms without being automatically enchanted by the arbitrary. Meaning is here, saturating the lines: this is not meaning like a kite with its neat string of explication attached; neither is it rote repudiation. Many of the poems are exquisite spacially: Fisher likes to use the whole page; her descending accruing shapes mime the sensations of associative thought—phrases seem to flood in from different parts of the mind, different parts of the life. The effect is musical, like the winds taking over from the strings.

This impression is fundamental. A highly trained, probing intelligence shapes this work, accounts for its precision, its shimmering logic that seems to belong more to mathematics than to language. And yet always the crucial impulse of these poems seems not argument but song. In *Frail-Craft*, Fisher has found a way to represent the cascade of sensations we think of as being without slighting the great presences, love and loss and death, that structure our perceptions. More impressively, she has found ways to generate emotional power without insisting on rigid correlation of event to insight. The marvel is how elegant, how whole, these poems are, their fluidity notwithstanding. Robert Hass has talked in this regard about rhythm as the underlying principle of form. His perceptions apply here; what gives Jessica Fisher's work its sense of form, of repose, is her perfection of ear. That repose, with its strange mobility, its accommodation of surprise, is Fisher's particular genius. To enter these poems is to be suspended in them: like dreams, they both surround and elude.

Repeated readings do not diminish this impression. I read *Frail-Craft* many times and felt, each time, the same involuntary relinquishing, the giving over, like someone standing at the edge of a body of water, hypnotized by the patterns of light, the slight shifts of color, and then led, without ever knowing how, deep into the recesses of contemplation, of emotion. The experience is unforgettable:

For a very long time   we'd been on the road, you bet

    we were tired of salt-beef, of sinew and the raw

                            wings of insects—

    and so I suppose you can imagine

                    how it felt at last

                              to cross the mountains

And when it's a long time

                    since you've slept

          in the disturbing softness

                              of someone's breath

that tree-body takes you by surprise—

                              space enough inside

               for most of us, yet

               all night we each felt all alone there

                                        walking

     from plain to peak to fog   toward the idea of ocean. . . .

                    "Stereography: Pioneer's Cabin, Near Grove"

                                        —Louise Glück

ACKNOWLEDGMENTS

Thanks to my family, friends, and teachers, and especially to Julie Carr, Ann Fisher-Wirth, Louise Glück, Robert Hass, Lyn Hejinian, Brenda Hillman, and Margaret Ronda. Their inspiring example and untiring engagement made this a better book.

Grateful acknowledgment is made to the editors of the following publications in which the following poems, sometimes in slightly different form, first appeared:
Five Fingers Review: Sun Tunnels, Brancusi's Heads
The New Yorker: The Right to Pleasure
The Threepenny Review: The Promise of Nostos

1

JOURNEY

Because the valley spreads wide, ridged with the signs
we read; or because what we needed was always at hand—
reach down and there was a book, there a slipper, there a glass
of ice cold water. Hopefully we walked
the paths laid before us, there was a burr-bush,
there a blue jay, quail and other creatures, too many
to follow. Where did they go once we lost their lead?
Which is to say, where did we not go? Quick, quick,
they called to us, but we heard only the sound
of our boots on dried leaves, and were mesmerized;
we spoke to one another of things in the path,
we chucked to our horses, when we had them,
and when we had hats we took them in our hands
and hallooed to the passersby (brahma bull, bright
green bird) though we were not yet out of the wood,
instead it closed in around us, deep were its streams
and the trees thick around and thick together, and we
were lost and led our horses and called out for a guide
until our voices grew rough and we decided we'd better
save them. We tried to climb to a loft in the branches,
being wary of night's prowlers, but the trunk tore our hands
and we bedded down in a hollow, the horses' quiet whinny
our lullaby. And what do you think we dreamt, there in
the forest with no voice left to call with? We dreamt
of the spread palm of the valley, of the path that led
from ridge to ridge, past elation, and then into the forest.

LULLABY

Sleep falls like
rain from dream

                              where once
                              I mothered
                              my mother
                        held her on my hip
                           at the brink
                        of the crashing sea
                          said Look Annie
                            it's a boat
                          meant Look Annie
                              our boat

        Über allen Gipfeln ist Ruh'
        Jeck was fool to think it
                    (the flame is blue
            where the fire burns hottest)

Searching for blindness
            source unknown & coda unwritten
                    she'll climb the dizzying stair
            to 26 Hybernská #3
where Čepina Sirová has written a poem:
        the puppy has spleen
                    because his mother dog got spots

                              We must board
                            and you will cry
                            as the dark sea
                          cradles you through
                            the nightmare
                          in which you touch
                            the fire's core

        the storm wakes you and naked you rise
        to move from warmth to wind & rain

                    Above the rooftops, thunder

LOVE'S VICISSITUDES

First you were hungry, then you were in love
and thought everything had changed, oh the sun
and the birds hidden in the trees, their presence
proved by singing. Happiness, you thought,
was given freely, the balance books
with their neat columns and faux leather covers
had nothing to do with it: this was not
like a wartime grocery, everything given
but on the short leash of credit. Abundance
and glory: that's it, it's been here all along
and as in the song the lovers sing as they cross the bridge,
you just didn't see it, didn't hear it, before.
You are willing to believe in a world where violins
begin to bow of their own accord, where a phrase
turns into a refrain and everything rhymes. Go ahead,
ridiculous one, say it's the springtime of the heart.

First you were hungry. Then you were in love.
Miraculous transformation, the path between
a labyrinth. Once you walk blinking
into the sudden sun, know the two will always
be twined. It is an outrage and you are outrageous
in your failure to distinguish between what ought
to be opposites, love and hatred, for example.

A RIDDLE FOR THE BODY

What *belong* means—

first question
            and first sorrow.

What comes into the mind and sets up shop
as truth, unrattleable, sure as sugar is not salt

            (that your body isn't yours
            wasn't yours to give away)

and all that thus far hasn't bothered
to make itself known appears,

pilots finally quiet, Klamath Lake,
Crater Lake, the Columbia River like

a disjointed finger, past Portland fog
and finally the sea, and the sentence enters

Beneath us is ocean, the children have perished—

but because the river leads
away from the source, moves

toward open water, the ocean's
swell and break will never lead back home,

and though it would be now or later—
the boat leaving port, waves taking the bow—

if you don't know where your body belongs,
you will bring sorrow, and if you don't

know to whom, it will be worse—

            What do you have to say about that?

NONSIGHT

1. *SPIRAL JETTY*

Light on water isn't a *thing*

though it lures the fragile eye
toward blindness

glints along the line that links
body to the disembodied—

The jetty begins underwater, reaches
the unfortunate, unseen ground;

the jetty *is* underwater—

we followed the shimmer of mica
because the account of their camp
had mentioned a quarry;
waist-deep in water, we swore we felt
the mounded stones.

What the jetty is like—
gone, because the beloved is gone—

What would you see, if you saw it? a stone, stones,
desire's dizzy spiral, that leads from ground
into the groundless, the deep, the windy water.

Site: where the particular falls—

but it was not here
he fell—

nothing
to recommend
this place

nothing here—

a ghost town

down the road, a bar,
the one motel

and yet here's as good as any
since *site* first meant sorrow,
grief, trouble of any kind—

here's all kinds:
heat and wind and cold,
land parched until the floods

but how to frame the view
on nothing—

a concrete channel

apertures for the sun—
and for the eye

a lens to pry it open—

3. CANAL

Because, despite the eye's illusion, parallel lines do not converge: so it was that we walked the canal in tandem, you on the north side, I on the south. I watched as you stooped to fix your shoe, as you took off your jacket, then put it back on again; I knew you were cold, too, when the wind came, and the rains, and then snow, sleet, hail—such offense taken, though there never was a crime, never the imagined tryst in the summer canal, our bodies pale against the nightblack reeds. But if the eye can love—and it can, it does—then I held you and was held.

MEMORY BURN

What relation has truth to this: morning and you're holding me, morning and you've gone? To work, and yet the heart welts.

 Words we need in our language:
 damals, Einmalig

although I don't remember who spoke, who was silent. I don't remember what the one who spoke said. I don't remember our room, but there were dolls, a trundle bed, a child with scarlet fever. It did not blind her, though I wanted to be the sister of a blind girl, I wanted to be the eyes through which she saw.

 There was a gash in my leg, that I can say truly, I still see the scar.

Although here and now is the medium you move through, then and then is the time of your verbs, every one of them conjugated, forgetful of the infinite which was their tense when they began and which they yearn for.

JUNE

Most unfathomable, that my mother once lay with you
in this room or that, knew your knees and palms,
each and every story of each and every scar—

to see you sitting side by side on her back porch,
eyes averted, tension in your shoulders, a parley
between rivals tired of war, splitting the kingdom.

If you hit, who you fucked, is not my business.
My business is to imagine the sweat of a June bed,
your bodies touching, fervent, then at rest;

my business is to stoke that fire, though what I remember
is the door locked in the storm, someone yelling,
and the years of trying to wade through two versions

of fourteen years, time during which I was nothing,
then a dream, then vision coming clearer. Then
prosecutor, judge: tell me did you, tell me did you,

and finally struck at your amazement. But I want
to think that what happened doesn't matter now,
so long as I can imagine June in a valley at the foothills,

a double bed in a small green clapboard house,
a child almost two sleeping in the next room,
and while the night brings cool, the bed is hot.

THE BORROWED DOOR

1. CASTAWAY

It began with a lesson: how to listen.

> Then, the chorus, a *brouhaha*
> > as they taught me to call it, but it was only
> the dogs, the birds, I understood.

The latter were kind to me, after a fashion,
when I couldn't decide what to wear,
> having lost my suitcase.

> Though my host still had a taste
> > for the exotic *contrapposto*,
> for the frame that opened onto the open secret

> > it was the double image
> > > that entranced—

we fought for our own reflections
in the foggy bathroom mirror
> though even our names rhymed

> > > and took turns
> > wearing the green sweater,
> > > the incredible feathered hat

and fell in love with versions
> of the same man,
> > according to the pact.

So I found myself
        in castaway clothes,
a prêt-à-porter that led me through
            a borrowed door

                    into the high-hedged
                garden's long alleys, halls
                        that looked like the halls before.

2. INSCAPE

The bottle's label peels; pears on the table turn toward the sun. And in the
cities of dead

      —no, they are singing. Rain slicks the pavement with sky, stone hums
in the heat, and you'd like to be able to say *one of these, please*:

          avec ceci, a body
        of which one might say, *ici suis-je—*

     curve of the breast in brushed velvet
          beside the generic shapes:

   red triangle, the black square.

        The reflection suggests

        that there should be address.
        Otherwise, why the black dress?

3. MISLAID

I knew how to ask directions
to only one place
and that's where I went

but words that might have been puns
flooded the living room

and on the coffee table
the tureen and sugarbowl were arranged
as a skull, the hinged jaw unhinging

we made tea
for people who never came

we drank it

Now—the parade. Lions, red, black & yellow. They *never* go anywhere without a drummer, & also have someone to carry extra oranges, & a hat carrier, for when they're tired. If their heads are bare they can be bonked with a stick. A few of them are even beginning to sprout some whiskers, which makes them grown up and disconcerting. Pierrot, little Gilles, les Paysans, les Marins—they're forever stopping, forming circles, sort of like puppets. They never walk—always this little dance. Even some babies take part—those with rich parents I guess. Then all the baskets are empty and supplies are gone.

A one-sided travesty. I hope we make it.

A most un-like non-grey color— We are dedicated to the Fat. Ann let me teach her the moves—that takes up time too. In real life, this house needs cleaning.

My interest and tolerance for family things is very high. In another way it is good. Whatever the balance, one would enjoy the things we would dig. I find whole periods of your histories, mom and dad, or Lockheed or Bakersfield.

I think it's a neat place, especially when you see all the neat things.

I suggest it would be excellent to get back in the habit of discriminatory viewing. How children their ages acted in another age, self-image at the expense of love. For the same reason, if the riots occur I don't want to be there, because of my feet.

I spend the time contemplating my essentially dirty nature—it probably surprises you not. Primarily because of gravity—though even that constant has its problems. Which brings us to the point of fact that today this house needs cleaning.

Distinctions in values desired and values attainable:

Though I will allow you to draw your own conclusion on the above, I am compelled to tell you that yesterday the sun shone. Mounted police forced the dancers off the street. Really exciting. All the windows in the town were covered with screening for that very event. A good time was had by all. Good dinner, good people, good night.

2

THE WEDDING

A boy stands at the edge of the water. He wears a plastic bag over his head, it's sealed at the neck. He thinks he'll be able to breathe underwater; he's wrong. He will drown when he jumps, he cannot swim.

A couple calls to me— quick, we've seen a girl, she's by the water, she's timid like an animal. But I'm telling my father and aunts to go buy votives, soon it will be dark, the store closes soon. They are a hundred for $8 or maybe a hundred for $4—either way a better deal than you'll find elsewhere.

Before jumping the boy waves his arms like wings. He is mad, he thinks Look! I'm a bird. I am a diver with my face mask & air tube. Now he is dead. But the girl isn't dead: she's scared. I follow the couple to where they glimpsed her; halfway through the tunnel I see her cowering, though I don't think she sees me. I feign exhaustion, take my foot in my hand, drop something for her to eat, she's so thin. She takes it, takes a long time to eat it—it's a Jolly Rancher, a watermelon one.

It's a wedding but the children are dying; I'm trying to help but I haven't a clue, I can't keep them merry, can't keep them from leaping. But this girl eats my candy; she's scared but not of me.

He's belly-down in the nest you've made on the floor in the add-on that was my room when I was small; the door is open so you can keep an eye on him. He's tuckered out from the move or whatever it is you went through before you arrived here, but his back is taut as a racehorse's haunches. No child sleeps like that, I should know. He's crying; I curl myself around him, ask what it is, I hate her, I hate her, through the shut doors we can hear the whack and laughter, he knows what it is.

THREE DREAMS

The bald eagle circled there, a papa eagle, inept at nest-making, but the eggs had lost their nest, and there was nothing else for him to do than to try to build a new one around them. They were so hard to contain, his would-be chicks, their shells were cracked open, no nest could house them, and still he circled with straws in his beak to make a bed for his would-have-been chicks. And I knew my brother was in danger.

I was turning the bend of a village road when a man in a VW bus pulled up beside and showed me a photograph of a boy with a blood-covered face. Do you know this man? he asked and my eyes told him yes he's my brother though what I said was that I had seen him before, I'd dropped him off at the bus stop where he had begun the journey to a place he'd never arrived. They've found him, he said, he was tortured, he's in the house just beyond. I burst into a room where men sat quiet at a table, my brother was not among them. He's in the other room, said the youngest, who was my other brother, and there I found him, eyes wide open but glassy, and when I took him in my arms he was so small, but still a man whose eyes had seen what they had seen. It was then I could not stand it, with that gangly body limp in my arms and every part of it in need of coaxing back. Then the scene changed to text in a book, and I was just reading, no longer afraid, and I thought Now that was clever, what a cheap shot—if it disturbs you, you don't have to look; if it disturbs you, make it a book.

I have almost reached him, the journey has been long but I'm in the right town at least, in my hometown. I call for directions, on the other line is a person trying to discern exactly where I am, giving landmark after landmark that will guide me to him. May I speak with him? I ask and when he comes on he says I am not well and I ask Where are you in relation to the white house with the topiaries? I'm just at the end of that block, he says, and I hang up and drop my backpack behind a tree because it would slow me. I might have been too late, but here I am running north on College, past homes on either side that used to house friends, and then I'm with him, but he is not well and our father doesn't know to come though he's less than an hour away. I want to call him, but my brother wants our father's travels to be lighthearted, and after all, we are in our own hometown, and should not all, then, of its own accord be well?

DREAM FOR MY OTHER BROTHER

Dropping you at school I saw
a man lurking where the children enter
and when he took you to the van
I made him see that I had seen him
and so he took me too. We were
afraid, but you more so, being younger,
and so I played you over the cell phone
the message in her voice, the movement
away from the mother countered then
by whatever words she thought to leave there,
and I sotto voce knew what to tell you: not Cry,
stolen child but Steel yourself against this.
You see I fear for both my brothers,
will follow them to danger—

ERRATA

I knew he was in danger
because he was both the egg
and the one who cracked it—

THE RESIDUAL

        —wherever you go, to the islands
or Glendale, wherever you go it's the same,
socks too big and stiff when the sweat dries.
Take on a man's body if you will, chest
and straight, but you're no different now
than you were when you climbed out of the bath
and out the window onto the roof
and huddled naked, lord of yourself—

TEN BOATS

One troupe is composed of the corpses of camels. I counted 180 heads and 304 feet. If a camel has one hump and a dromedary two, how many will have perished at the mirage?

The earth turns the sun around: one by one rejections that we suffered come full circle, and therefore the refracted rays are immeasurable, multicolored in the eye's kaleidoscope. Tell me what distance the earth, and the perimeter of her ruffled skirts! and suppose that the remarriage theme superseded courtship day by day, until at the end of a hundred, it had eclipsed its light.

To carry a million apples, you'd need a train with quite a wagon. If the train were long, would the wagon be longed for? Or, is the apple among the big and little numbers?

Admittedly, in a favorable climate, the number of boatmen corresponds to the hours. But at the end of experience, there is a chrysalis with ten boats. How many are there on the fourth day, supposing that each has the form of a bullet, and is as long as your thumbnail, and as wide—?

LOVE CRIED ME A RIVER

Love cried me a river, sang me a song. Nice song, lots of notes. I did not draw them. I tossed a quarter in the air and down it came, lo and behold. We weren't happy but we sang anyway, her sandals tied around her ankles, and I thought love must be like that, taut but yielding.

Say now what you wanted to hear, and don't perch there on the rockiest spot in the whole garden, the column's edge like a blade in your spine. There are loveseats and flowers, a long alley to either side, somewhere for the eye to roam, and if it doesn't feel like roaming, then let it focus here, where children push boats with long sticks.

You don't have to know love to taste the orange, but there was a great tree whose roots reached down the cliffside, and beyond it we could count the fishing boats and the men on each, we watched as they threw their nets out but couldn't see what they caught—

LOVE LETTER

We were gardening, then you were gone, though the seedlings still had to be planted, and I figured you had gone to make us tea. You took a long time, though, and I thought who does he think he is, leaving it all to me?

I went in. I wasn't allowed to see you, though I knew you'd still be in your triple-stitched Carhartts with dirt perennially in the half-dozen pockets, and yet it was I who had seen first where we were headed, in the valley, a long way down. I knew we would reach it on foot though we might as well take the train, because of the cold and the distance and the late hour of the day. All that, and the visions you brought me, gone. I wished for it back then, even if only our fights in the basement.

THE SERMON

A long man came on foot, his hair was long too. He spoke above the river. Many people came, so many that his voice couldn't reach them all, but I heard it: I climbed a tree just behind.

Below me, a woman got to her knees and cried, her hair was thin as a bird's first feathers, her mouth made a horrible shape. Mother said she must be a sinner, that the words of this man, who has held the Christ, pricked her soul like a needle does cloth.

I didn't cry, nor did Daan Nachtegaal—he was in the tree too. After the man finished we went back to swordfighting. The sinners followed him into the river and drowned.

THE CHANGE

And there we were, paddling, terrified
and where the dam broke, just inches away
wanting to say it's not me in this boat
I oughtn't be rowing I ought to be sleeping—

FLAYED

           —the dream I stayed with past waking
in which Pascale sits sewing rabbit fur to glove your hands
and silently, feet propped on a table, I flay a long strip
from each thigh to make you boots. The skin peels easily,
it's like stripping the pale bark from a fallen birch,
the muscle beneath like the crimson trunk still teeming,
but I can't believe I could even dream it, who vomited
in the museum bathroom at Bruges after seeing the four-
paneled painting of the lawyer skinned for lying in court.
I imagined them salting his flesh, needling it, excited
in their cruelty. Why I thought you'd want these boots
I don't know, unless as evidence that this body is yours still.

3

FRAIL-CRAFT

It's a true story: we were at sea, together at risk,
and he was very poor, a regular fisherman, from
a family of such. He happened to fill the equation
in the geometry of appetite I trace: for even the blind
can see! And so you see it's not so much about the eye
as whatever is made to serve the master who asks
for wine, wants the pickled *fruits de mer* alongside
the treatise on navigation and the maps that show
what oceans hide.

                 Yet men still drown
in order to know the difference between sky
and whatever name you give to the deep. Otherwise
they see the sea as surface, want to sit on the beach
and say Look at me, looking at the sea!

WATER, VODA

—in memory of Zdenek Sirový

≡

Wherever trees gather their leaves into red and gold and the sky is washed with the hillside's green, there you are;

and here beneath, where the podvodníci cower, in the deep waters we came to, drawn by the promise of blue your eyes made;

forced to drink what you called "little water," and Becherovka, and coffee, the grounds of which sat for days with coarse beet sugar in the cups' bottoms, so many of them in their little corner I didn't know where to begin, the faucet broken, bath water rusted, groaning through the pipes—

Moonless first night of the year, sparklers thrown high into birch trees, and you led me through the frozen forest to the corner in the barren yard beside the herringbone stone wall, and laughing said here you'd lay it down—

≡

He's telling me you're dead
    but he gets so close we're kissing
she's telling me you're dead
    but we're running across harvested fields
    and she's ahead and the wind is unfaithful
        I hear her say that because it's winter
        we should hide salt in the forest—

≡

The little underwatermen   (rowing, your oar
                 might smack one)   of the
fugitive red underpainting

    sky filched from the meadow,
    the sun cast a watery green:

        even now, in dream,
        the fox has a blackbird by the wing

                and she is on fire.

More like an angel than architecture now,
bird that flew by and did you see it?
Certain prophet, husbandman, great
task-master, I missed both experience
and meaning. Fire and flaumbe on al the town
shal sprede, yet astronomy tells me nothing
of you. Shards among the strata, the excavation
gone all wrong, a gold-filled tooth taken to mean
Don't cry. Sap, oh and I'm sorry to see it,
the latest American barbarism, charming interpolation,
when all I know to be true is that you were
as straight as a dig, and though one thing
leads to another, nothing leads to you.
Neither now nor to come, though the swain,
the seamen, and the seven wait. Here are doves, diggs,
drakes, redshankes, running through the lakes: hear them.

SONG

Where were we headed, following that voice—

an outing to hear the nightingale: we stood in a field
that bordered the forest

dusk; we knew we wouldn't see it singing

bored, actually, in that soggy field
we waited a long time

And if you didn't feel the lure of the song? It was dusk, cold already, the field was
soggy, the company strange, each wanting to be enraptured, not wanting to
talk, and the song faraway still, and then gone again, and again we waited for
night and the nightingale, thinking of death and the lyric—   or not—

thinking why should the bird be taken as a sign, and
what the meaning of the sign should be—   so rudely forced—

bored, actually, with the logic of signs
and bored with the nightingale's song

we couldn't see it,
not that sight would have been
the difference we sought—

NOVELLA

1.

Seated in the choir, I waited for a friend who never came, studying the women's hats until the bell rang for recess. He wasn't on the playground, either, not hiding in the tree.

Back in class I told the teacher that the outcome of the battle hadn't been good for either side, not wanting to cast my vote with the victor. But I was thinking all the while of François, who would, I imagined, have made off for the woods, looking again for whatever he'd seen. Like trying to find a passage in a book, he'd said, when you remember only that it was in the middle somewhere. *Where* is the question of the mysterious domain, addressed in the fourth section of the second part. What you find when you're lost you can't look for, I'd argued: you'd have to get lost to find it again.

Stupid thing to have said, though it was true. And where did I first glimpse him? On the stairs, running to recess? or at prayer, among the nuns in their dark hoods? He'd touched the back of his neck, where my eyes had fallen, and it was like his name, which fit like a glove you'd outgrown, then worn through the wet afternoon—

Taking dictation, my pencil slipped. She asked me to copy my errors; I watched as they grew. Say each twenty times and it's yours, she said. Madame, I replied, I cannot speak these words: they belong to the page, and will not come off of it, to sit on my tongue. I knew better than to lick the book. As punishment for being tight-lipped, I had to sit at my desk as the children cleared away, writing words in rows.

What I stole, I kept: these few mistaken phrases, jotted in the margins. Though the passage at hand described raucous men at long tables, drunken after the harvest, from the very first lines, I was prepared for a tormented story. How could it be otherwise, when François, who loved that book, had disappeared from the grounds like a minor character who knocks only once at the door—

What the book meant, I wrote, was that the pleasures of a peasant childhood, which we had thought promised, were not ours any longer. There would be no candle left burning in the window, for the lover home from war or the traveler lost in the night. How, then, was François to find his way, given that the lakes, scattered through our district, each looked like the next, and their banks turned to marshland in the spring thaw? His footsteps, left on the ice, would be gone when he went to retrace them.

I resolved then and there to leave the signs he would seek, looking for a way home: a red ribbon tied to a twig might catch his eye from a distance, and would be like the voice that calls out at dusk, Over here!

3

Sudden rain: there was nowhere to go but into the library, where the shelves bowed with the weight of old books. I pulled one down—a story in which the mother fails to come to the gate. The rhetoric was simple and struck me as dull, like vegetables grown in an overwatered garden. Whether the story mentioned her thwarted love didn't matter: by tuberculosis or arsenic, the end was the same. In the next, requited love made impossible by conscription or travel, the long wait and, finally, a reunion in the churchyard, blossoms woven into the bride's hair. In a third, the village pastor. The next spoke of friendship that couldn't survive love; the fifth reminded, in allegorical terms, that you can't judge a book by its cover. Nowhere could I find the story that I craved, that would describe nothing in great detail.

I began to think that the incredible boredom of reading, like pacing a hall waiting for the appointed time, was, in fact, foreseen: why else the delineated words, which might have been scattered like sandpipers on a beach, their bodies, their shadows, and their tracks all caught in the eye's first glance. Perhaps, I thought, the door will never open—what then of your patience, and of the pleasure you learned to take in the sound of your footsteps?

I consulted the card catalogue and found it incomplete: there was nothing at all under the heading "François, love of," and when pressed, the librarian said she thought such a thing didn't exist, or else it would be listed, there between *France* and *Franconia*. In the end, I waited out the storm flipping through *A Geography of the Lake Region in Pictures and Prose*; it was, in short, a summation of the place I held dear because of François, which remains, though he's gone, like the paper beneath the march of these letters. . . .

Where I looked for him? In the gardens and grounds to the south, that formed backdrop to our games of hide and seek: that, I imagined, was where he'd go if he wanted to be found. To the north, across the cattle guard, along the road that led toward war; he would have made a dapper soldier. And in the roadside gullies—I couldn't help but think of some misadventure, of the word *befall* with its archaic premonitions, of the blind man who trails the voyager begging for coins or bread. I tried instead to think of the circus: of the way the town's heart shifted when the market was displaced by the striped tent with its three turrets, its red flags riding high as the steeple; of the lion-tamer's approach to danger, his carriage erect amidst the flaming hoops, the feral beast circling where he stood—

But like the circus, which had been everything to us all summer, from dawn when we pitched hay to the acrobat's horse, to dusk when she sewed the loose spangles back on her skirt, François was gone. On Saturdays the market took over what I had come to think of as the circus grounds, and if there was a spangle left glinting in the gravel, I never saw it. *Without a trace* is the phrase that comes to mind when I think of what is gone, though most of what goes returns: summer, the circus. Once I thought I glimpsed him through the windows of the prefecture, its red shutters latched open like the lobes of his heart; another time I would have sworn I heard his voice rising above the others in the choir; and where the cattails were flattened, there he must have lain, I mused as I sat fishing the third lake on the outskirts of town.

Though the past is like a stone thrown into the lake, there but irretrievable, still, years later, stumbling in the gallery of pictures upon *Souvenir de Mortefontaine*, painted when we were children there, I got a chill up my spine as if, on the other side of the lake from where the boat drifts, we're still tying flies or gutting the trout we caught. And standing there, a velvet rope delineating the distance between where I was and where I had been, I felt like the fish that went for the fake, its innards, its still-beating heart, tossed into the trees where the birds waited to feed. What was it about that picture, I wondered, the paint inert upon the canvas? *Souvenir* indeed: a worthless thing you take away, and treasure.

5.

Because alone on the road, reading the signs, even a stone in the shoe displaces thought, I forgot that the point of the hunt is to capture what flees,

but if the heart is a ribbon I tied to the branch, and the hawk perching there pecks twice and takes flight, his appetite whet,

then to hunt is to wait for the bells of the tiercel, bloody with quarry—

I'd borrowed a book that told of such guides as can find what you've lost, be it a ring off your finger or the beloved who is gone,

but my eyes grew heavy as I started to read, the book propped on the pillow where I lay down my head,

and I scaled the side of the mountain to steal an eyas from the falcon's nest, rappelling back down as the book hit the floor:

I wanted the bird that returns to be mine, the hunt a mere pretext to send him away—

6.

I listened to the rain on the tiles of the house where vacations once led me as if I were a foundling. That's one word in my particular vocabulary that I use to mark my homecoming to my country home, the welcome it gives me and that's never as it was. Every such house has a tiled roof and tiled floors: that's a given. But what has become of the hidden notes that told me where to find my pleasure, hiding in the garden rows or in the fifth-floor closet? Which is to say, what has become of François, for whom night was a nightingale and day the daylily?

If there were a maze with François at its center, like the liquor hidden in the chocolates he smuggled, then the book would remain unwritten, unread, and I would ride fast down the elm-lined alleys, looking for where the underbrush broke. If I had a hound, unleashed, on his scent; if there were a priest, a pulpit, a prayer; if I knew a song that would sing me to sleep, then François would be waiting at the end of the road, at the edge of the forest, tangled in bracken, drunk on the berries that hang there like bells—

THE PROMISE OF NOSTOS

The sea is not bent on circularity: it says *Here is an island,*
anchor here.
                    But because love waits, the broken hull
is soon patched, a torn sail sewn to hold the wind,
and then once again they set course. The uncalled for jubilance
at departure, feigned tears, the make-believe dream
where so-and-so appeared to say fly away home.
They do not leave for home. They do not leave to return,
despite their promises. They leave to leave, and if I love them
it's because they come hungry as a dream, and like a dream
their stay distills a life, or what a life could be—

THE RIGHT TO PLEASURE

You would think that I go mad with grief
when the white sails fill and the keel cuts
the waters like a knife honed on whetstone:
that's the way you're taught to interpret these signs—
matted hair, the salt-dirt lines where sweat has run,
hands that feed the mouth but will not wipe it.
But when my love decides to go and then is gone,
I can still taste him, bitter in the throat; I still
feel the weight of his body as he fights sleep.
I do not fight it: on the contrary, I live there,
and what you see in me that you think grief
is the refusal to wake, that is to say, is pleasure:
qui donne du plaisir en a, and so if
when he couldn't sleep in that long still night
you sensed it and woke to show him how
to unfasten each and every button, then it is
promised you, even when he goes—

TIDE

≡

In your absence there was a flower, an iris there by the sea,
and so I was for once not thinking that any minute it might
drag you under. Because of the flower, the sea was backdrop only,
dusky gray to set its violet burning. You were of course
always in my heart, but it was in my eye, was its very color.

≡

Deep water, sorrow, and why?

But even for the prisoner shackled where seawater washes
twice a day at high tide, the torture is not, I think,
in the fact of the tide, since its rising and falling
is sign of nothing but movement without determination,
of a course that is set and so is run, for no other reason.

≡

Nothing changed, but when you came to me and traced along my shoulders
until the lines of your tracing met at mid-spine, there was so clearly then
a dress of black shimmering feathers, in straps that widened to cover
the breasts, to cover the blades that sprang as wings there, and I was then
sorrow's blossoming, abundant as nighttime, radiant in mourning.

RECKLESS

Nothing counters sorrow: it drives it
says careful now down the twisted streets
but when it takes the wheel, you'll know danger:

                    the queen has her petticoats as the sky has its clouds,
                         as the clouds grow from the gray skin skimmed
                    to snakeskin dyed the hues of fuchsia: here melon, here mauve,
                    as when gray takes what's given, and rakes the given sky—

BRANCUSI'S HEADS

          —what brings me back
is resting my cheek in your hand,

like the small ovals Brancusi carved
from marble for the blind to see,

heads that, held until the cold weight
warmed, then laid back down, might

sway a while until they found again
that stillness of the tipped skull, cupped.

4

DEBATE

1. CONJECTURE

Door opens and you slam it closed. What was it you saw?
Six brides burning—like chimes they turned, oh and the sound!
Taken to mean the man's not skilled in husbandry.
And out the window, something persists on the horizon:
a fin in the waste of water; or someone's hand, too tired to wave.
The eye is a roving light, it wants what it sees, and is what it wants.
But if it didn't take the shape of a wolf, prowler;
if the wolf lay down, lean and lonely, and slept—

2. AGAINST CONJECTURE

Bit of light glinting on the sea: that's all I see,
and not, as you say, duck or drake, girl or gull,
Jessica or drowned, but to say she rode the waves
is to tell another kind of story, with a rhythm, not a plot.

> (It seemed clear as water in a glass
> that you did not love me, but what is love
> if not recognition despite disguise?)

Plain as a penny, copper, dapper,
or buried as an unconformity,
in the eyes of the stray ribbed with hunger,
every delve of the spade means love.

> Little wonder that in the sunshine,
> in the garden, your eyes turn to the ground
> you dig, but leave the bones buried.

THE INDISTINGUISHABILITY OF BROTHERS

Not revenge for all your small misdeeds, not for lack of love
for you, but because the night was very hot, humid and close,
because we drank red wine on the beach, not meaning it preface
to anything at all, certainly not to those four legs flailing, sand
everywhere, days afterward still working itself free from the scalp.
That was to be sign of my shame, the sand that wouldn't wash out,
and I knew for once the fear of the bride who scours the stain
from one side of the key, only to find it's moved to the other.

Here there is nothing to break the hush, you do not ask and I do not tell
but sand falls onto my shoulders, into the soup, and at supper
nothing softens the crust of the bread, it sticks in my throat
like the crafted defense I want for you to hear. Neither for revenge
nor for lack of love, but because love deep as this sees the beloved
wherever it looks. It's true in all the tales, I could cite a hundred.
I would, the lover says, know you anywhere, your hair dyed black
or red, in cowl and hood or changed into a nightingale, wherever
you went I would seek you. Forgive me then this my crime:
that in my desire for you, I saw you where you were not.

READING TO KNOW YOU

Fissured cup that neither leaks nor breaks, leaks but does not break, breaks, or a phrase in Latin, a construction never taught you, *the soldiers being tired*;

and since to hold your beauty would be to hold it still, I can't tell you that I read Woolf to know you, Flor de Caña spiking my Coke, Jacqueline sweeping mostly to be near,

when the closest I can get is the *Yes, if, but* or something to do with Bœuf en Daube, the whole thing spoilt with saying it would not be fine, with a hand taking a pear—

still life forced onward, so that the arrested eye is taught to take its own revenge, yet in the end the body knows the change, but cannot show it. Therefore there's no error in the nonsense syntax:

Mr. Ramsay stumbling along a passage stretched his arms out one dark morning, but, Mrs. Ramsay having died rather suddenly the night before, he stretched his arms out.

MY RUSSIAN LULLABY

That wolves sleep, though they hunger,
is little comfort. Snow falls on snow,
furious for white, still it is the craving
that marks you, you are not numb
but stunned by sorrow, every nook
and cranny of its shop of signs crammed full,
and sorrow is to you as the dog is to the bone:
worrying a dead thing, or a thing that wants
to be let alone, to sleep until the hunger passes.

THE HUNGER FOR FORM

Sidewinder's trail in the windswept desert, that's how I saw

the snaking hairs leading down—

I'd not yet been there, I did not know how makeshift the rim.

If you sit in the front row
then you are on stage

if you see blood on the glass
then you have chosen blood

and because matter hungers for form, from form into form it passed—

Dragon of Love, love's devourer
hunger has an end:

here it is

the winding path
come full stop

.

what sand conceals it will reveal, in the wind

STEREOGRAPHY

> Extremes meet. Every given point of the picture is as far from
> the truth as a lie can be. But in travelling away from the pattern
> it has gone round a complete circle, and is at once as remote
> from Nature and as near it as possible.
>
> Oliver Wendell Holmes
> "The Stereoscope and the Stereograph"
> *The Atlantic Monthly*, 1859

STEREOSCOPE FOR THE 29ᵀᴴ BATHER

a box to hold the unmoored gaze   drifting on the water

but no more illusion   than the world as vision gives it

("in the round")   to the imagined eye—

the sectioned orange   unconsumed—

the water deep   where doubled—

unwet—   appetite—

where eye meets eye   by the waterside—

Riverway lined with branches
insubstantial

lit in the morning, lit at dusk

and to see our ship! you'd think it a tree,
filigree moving down the waterway

Something caught,
broke,
fell into the water

and we watched it go,
followed its fall—
shimmering, electric—

unsure what it meant,
the mast gone,
our expedition lost—

Afterward I thought of where the river branched,
where it met a warming current

and we rode the waters
warm although in winter

2. DOWNSTREAM

Where the river led, we learned to follow:

        past fields, to where the fieldhands slept
                so tired they didn't hear us calling

    or were we underwater, and they awake there at the riverside
                  lunching,
                      jocular,
          whistling on reeds,
             chewing sweet clover,
                   sourgrass—

sons of Whitman, lolling—

as if a page torn from a picture book,
        the child too young to read,

                story followed after the eye
                   made whatever sense it could

3. AUGURY

One in our party trusted in birds:
        the red ones meant *Follow*

    but they flit from tree to tree
        in the light rain
        eating berries, the centers of flowers—

We studied them, seeking a code
        in their song,
        quarreled over the meaning—

What to say of what we saw,
        following the lead that led astray?
    They fought over the branch, the berries.

Eventually the damp got to us,
        and the not knowing
    what to make of them,

    but for a long time we watched
        their hot color flashing—

4. GORGE

When we woke we thought the world is a garden,

        which was how we imagined the dream, an inhabitability

    we dwelt in, or on, the way the eye learns to love

          what it sees, and is: green because a green day, blue

      blue, the illusion of depth becoming a gorge

    we stumbled into, and could not scale, or would not—

the gorge belonging, after all, to the river that made it,

      and the river shimmering with the granite's quartz,

    so that the question *Whose*, which defines us, is a riddle,

        the idea of a response in our minds as we walked,

           the long road ahead of us and the long road behind,

      through that freedom which depends on the dream

    where sight becomes home, the gorge hung with green,

        the river an afterthought—

5. VIEW FROM WESTERN SUMMIT

We were brought by story
    over ridge and valley

        and we took as our own
          granite and hunger

      dipped our hands in the cold stream
      drank of that water—

    Who was to say what to tell
      what to keep to ourselves—

Beauty was the guileful bait
      (river-rock, trout-lily)
to the eye at the edge

      Unobliged for any accident
(naufrage, burning)
    unless the hazard be taken

        but little bird, you walked
        right into the snare—

6. HALF STEREOGRAPH OF FALLEN LEAF LAKE

See they are already caught
in the still lake's surface

        their horses
        turn into it

            water
            emulsion

    how many
    would you say there are

           riding sidesaddle
           from the jagged shore

      and is the black
      blanket or dog?

For a very long time   we'd been on the road, you bet
     we were tired of salt-beef, of sinew and the raw
                                 wings of insects—
        and so I suppose you can imagine
                    how it felt at last
                        to cross the mountains

And when it's a long time
                since you've slept
       in the disturbing softness
                 of someone's breath
that tree-body takes you by surprise—
               space enough inside
        for most of us, yet
         all night we each felt all alone there
                         walking
   from plain to peak to fog   toward the idea of ocean

What dreams we'll leave you
               salmon runs
                   the idea
     of something outside:

      luminous patch of sky
    through branches & black needles

NOTES

LULLABY

The line in German, from Johann Wolfgang von Goethe's *Wandrers Nachtlied*, translates as "Above all the peaks is silence."

NONSIGHT

Spiral Jetty refers to Robert Smithson's 1970 earthwork, a black basalt spiral in the reddish water of Utah's Great Salt Lake. Just two years after its completion, an increase in the level of the lake submerged the jetty; it remained underwater for almost thirty years. Smithson died in 1973; three years later, his widow, Nancy Holt, created *Sun Tunnels* near the abandoned town of Lucin, Utah, more than a hundred miles southwest of *Spiral Jetty*. The installation consists of four concrete pipes arranged in an open X formation; each pipe is pierced with holes corresponding to the pattern of a celestial constellation.

MEMORY BURN

This poem borrows its title from Anne Carson's *Autobiography of Red*.

FRAIL—CRAFT

The opening lines of this poem paraphrase Jacques Lacan's story of boating with Petit-Jean in "The Line and the Light," from which the phrase "frail craft" also comes.

DEBATE

Virginia Woolf's vision of a "fin in the waste of water" served as the impulse for *The Waves*, a novel composed, she wrote, "to a rhythm and not to a plot" (diary, 7 February 1931; letter to Ethel Smyth, 28 August 1930).

Notes

THE HUNGER FOR FORM

Inspired by Fiona Shaw's performance as Medea, this poem derives two lines from Chaucer's account of Medea in *The Legend of Good Women* (lines 1580–1585).

STEREOGRAPHY

Stereography, from the Greek for "solid writing," describes the depiction of solid bodies on a plane. It usually refers to stereoscopy, which emerged in the 1840s in tandem with photography, thanks to the discovery that binocular vision enables our perception of depth. Because of the distance between the eyes, each sees a given scene differently. The mind, however, transposes the retinal images to an imaginary "cyclopean" eye in the center of the forehead, creating a single composite picture and interpreting the differences between the initial two images as depth. Likewise, the stereoscope combines two photographs, taken from slightly different points of view, to produce an illusion of three-dimensionality.